Excursions in Hypnagogia

by Kevin W Garrett

Table of Contents

Publishing Info

Excursions in Hypnagogia, copyright 2022 by Kevin W. Garrett. All rights reserved. No portion of this book may be reproduced, stored in a retrieval system, or transmitted, in any form or by any means—electronic, mechanical, photocopying, recording, or otherwise, without prior consent from the author and publisher.

The author of this book makes no warranty of any kind, express or implied. The author shall not be held liable in any event for the incidental or consequential damages in connection with, or arising out of, the furnishing, performance, or use of this information.

Illustrations, diagrams, covers, and book design by Kevin Garrett

Third Edition-print.

ISBN: 978-1-7375596-7-2

Changes from Prior Editions

New sections added or revised since the 1st Edition.

- Other Hypnagogic Sounds, p. 23
- Hypnagogic Waypoints, p. 29
- Hypnopompic Sounds, p. 33
- Hypnopompic Tripping, p. 34
- Collected Dreamlets (revised content), p. 39
- Familiarity (added content), p. 46
- Forgetfulness, p. 50
- Ignoring, p. 50
- The Dreamer's Age, p. 61
- Recurring Situational Themes, p. 67
- Index, p. 81

Changes from the 2nd Edition.

- Larger trim size
- New and different Hypnagogic Vocalizations
- Added Colophon, p. 80
- Minor edits
- Different ISBN

Introduction

Hypnagogia from the Greek, *hupnos* 'sleep' + *agō-gos* 'leading'—Leading to sleep.

Hypnagogia is the semi-waking-semi-sleeping twilight world that one experiences when falling asleep. Unless one is having trouble falling asleep, it is a most enjoyable state.

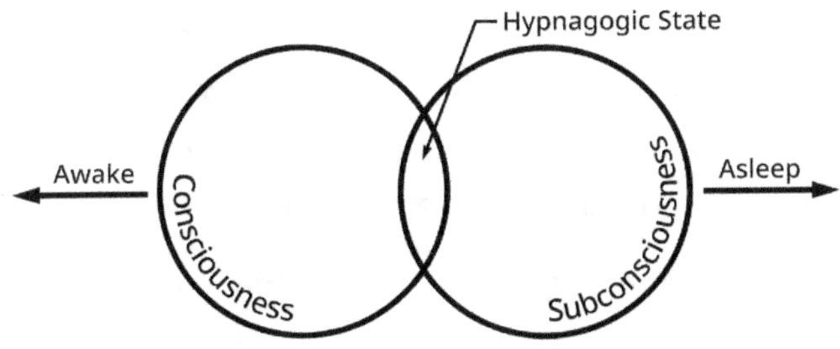

Figure 0.1 | The Hypnagogic State

Hypnopompia is the other end of sleeping—the semi-waking state when rousing into consciousness after sleeping. From the Greek, *hupnos* 'sleep' + *pompē* 'sending away'—Leading out of sleep.

Much of what is discussed in this book applies to both states, but primarily the hypnagogic state will be addressed. Dreams proper are also given attention in this work.

Throughout the book, I will usually use the term "dreaming mind" in lieu of "subconscious mind."

"Subconscious" is the usual term employed, but I prefer "dreaming mind," as we are talking about an area and situations in which one's awareness is not entirely subconscious—especially in waking hallucinations (see **Chapter 7 | Hallucinations, p. 70**).

In this book, I will present opinions that may, or may not, be in accordance with established research. These are my opinions. Very little of what you will find here is based on scientific research, but is instead based on *my own experiences and my conclusions as to their causes and meanings*. Frankly, I figure my guesses are as good as theirs.

I am *not* telling you what to think. I am telling you what *I* think.

Chapter 1 | Hypnagogic Physical Manifestations

Hypnagogic Myoclonus

Hypnagogic Myoclonus is the muscle twitching you sometimes get when falling asleep. Wikipedia calls it "Hypnic Jerk." Admittedly, three syllables are easier to say and write than eight.

Myoclonus from "myo" (muscle) and "clonus" ('violent, confused motion' or spasm)—An irregular muscle twitch. Presumably, the plural is "myocloni," although I find no evidence of that usage.

I first experienced hypnagogic myoclonus in the '80s when I'd lie down after work. It was always my right shoulder, which would jerk upwards. I was an engineer at the time, often working at a drafting board (positioned nearly vertically) most of the day. I think that myoclonus relieves built-up muscle tension.

So, what causes hypnagogic myoclonus? I think it's built-up electrical fields collapsing, sending electric currents to the muscles, causing them to move.

Hypnagogic myoclonus is surprising and often fun. I once had a hypnic jerk that resulted in both my arms being flung upwards towards the ceiling.

I had been lying on my back, and suddenly—both arms outstretched towards the sky, faster than I possibly could have willingly and seemingly with no effort. I laughed and laughed.

Over time, the muscles that experience myoclonus change. It is rare for me to have hypnic jerks in my legs, and never violently. It is most often in my shoulders. I went through a period of a double-myoclonus: one shoulder, then immediately the other. If lying on my back, it rocked my body back and forth.

For the last year or so, my typical hypnic jerk pulls both shoulders forwards, and my face scrunches up.

Wikipedia mentions that hypnic jerks can cause insomnia. Sure, it momentarily halts one's descent into sleep, but I've never found it to be an issue. In fact, I rather enjoy my hypnagogic myoclonus and miss it when it doesn't happen.

Hypnic Jerk at Wikipedia
[en.wikipedia.org/wiki/Hypnic_jerk]

Hypnagogia at Wikipedia
[en.wikipedia.org/wiki/Hypnagogia]

Exploding Head Syndrome

I have had "Exploding Head Syndrome," a condition in which the brain experiences a loud bang or exploding sound, with associated physical sensations in the head, while falling asleep.

Before I knew what it was called, my occurrences of exploding head syndrome were rather worrying. I asked a few doctors about it. Typically, they'd just stare at me with a blank expression, as if I had not even said anything. I was relieved and happy when I discovered that what I was experiencing had a name and that it was not dangerous or unhealthy.

Because of the similarities to hypnagogic myoclonus, I believe that exploding head syndrome is also built-up electrical fields collapsing, producing electric current, but in the brain instead of muscles. In other words, just like hypnagogic myoclonus, except in the brain.

It has been decades since I had a violent episode of exploding head syndrome. Every once in a while, I still get a minor version of the phenomenon. There will be what feels like a wave passing through my consciousness, which has a direction (usually from front to back), and a difficult-to-describe sensation in the brain. There will also be a sound—usually a dull, short roar, but sometimes a sound like a bell or the sound of hitting a damped drumhead.

Exploding Head Syndrome at Wikipedia [en.wikipedia.org/wiki/Exploding_head_syndrome]

Chapter 2 | Hypnagogic Mental Manifestations

As I have gained experience in the art of napping, I have grown more aware of what's going on in the twilight zone between wakefulness and sleep. Scenes and sounds begin to bubble up from the dreaming mind, most of which pass unnoticed and unremembered.

In the hypnagogic state, sounds and images originating in the subconscious mind may come to your conscious attention. These sounds and images may be the manifestation of a subconscious dream, but more likely, they are the germ from which a dream may grow.

Hypnagogic Sounds

I first became aware of what I call "hypnagogic vocalizations" about 10 to 12 years ago. I'd be falling asleep, and I'd notice sounds—usually spoken words. Sometimes in a woman's voice. Never my voice. What's going on here?

Apparently, what is going on, are random emanations from the dreaming mind (the subconscious) breaking through into consciousness. In the state of falling asleep—not engaged with reality and not actually asleep—one can become aware of sounds and sights created by the dreaming mind.

I have noticed that the sentences that come to my awareness are *occasionally* incomplete and that my semi-conscious mind attempts to mold them into proper sentences. So, maybe I get a subject, a verb, and an object, and I catch myself trying to fill in the rest to make sense of it.

Occasionally, words are unintelligible. After I think about what I heard, sometimes I manage to figure out what the unintelligible word or words were supposed to be. Except that they weren't supposed to be anything. They were just sounds, and my brain seeks to impose order upon them.

The voices are sometimes shouting. Not yelling, like someone angry, but shouting like Garrett Morris on the SNL News when he interpreted for the hard of hearing.

These hypnagogic vocalizations are usually distinct from dreamlets (p. 37). It's not like they're the soundtrack to the dream or dreamlet I'm having (or are they? See **Dreamlets and Hypnagogic Vocalizations, p. 43**).

Hypnagogic Vocalizations

These sentences and person names have no meaning. At least, I ascribe no meaning to them. More likely, they weren't even words (i.e., sounds representing meanings) but mostly sounds upon which my mind attempts to find meaning, and probably altering the sounds to fit.

If that were entirely true, however, they would not be in proper sentence structure, which they are, more often than not. It has been suggested to me that these vocalizations are playback of "recordings" of speech one has heard during the day, and the dreaming mind alters them.

I present here some collected vocalizations. There have been many more, but I'm not always in the mood to groggily use the voice recorder app on my phone to record them, and I can never remember them if I don't. They are ordered, more or less, in the order that I "received" them. My favorites are presented in **bold**.

Collected Sentences

Cut to hacks, Mr. Jones.

There are house plans for noobs now.

That's a four-legged donut. Be careful!

Don't worry, boys, Hugo will be there. He's a mensch! [1]

John and I made out… a set of ideas. [2]

Is it legal here?

Radi-Ant the Hoot wears a sad suit.

Sliced… and focussed… it goes up.

This kid got me by a ten-ounce floating off of the lamp rocket.

Sprinkler alienate soup.

Did you congratulate your head on your hair?

A young nephew who is startled by a child.

A bathtub scandal. You're trying to get a bathtub in your scandal.

I can paint roughnessssssss.

Oh… Let me throw the book at your face.

I mistook you for Andler Chambler.

If I cavitate, I freak.

I have my own knowledge. It's called "build."

The girl brings her sober either.

1. In the voice of an old Jewish man.

2. Female voice

Fine is to finger as steak is to tiger… Either the one.

It's a regular Isthisius.

Don't forget immediately, him having a gentle-man breakfast. [3]

He admitted it, but you'll never change your mind.

Associating with Dr. Genuine Father.

It was one of those case, where someone makes a k'shot. [sic]

Girls don't approach me on Tuesday.

It wasn't the Amigans who beat us—it was the Vegans.

"Where can I find it?" "Lost and Found." "Lost and Found?" [4]

He opened the door and said, "Here's the door that's open."

A long the shot—towards the very end. North of Fresno.

Push button. The Button Pushers.

---

3. Spoken in a thick, foreign accent

4. This is the only entry I have of a dialog between two people. I assume that it is me asking the question.

Chapter 2 | Hypnagogic Mental Manifestations

Under the purpose of law, the last person seen cleaning up the streets is…

It's a hoax near Doax.

Let's give Neptune an allowance.

Consue hubris.

A party of ungate significances. [5]

There's a bullet. Ninety watt!

It's like forceses.

The man is a Pullee—a Carishener.

Fending father? Or fending father accompaniment?

A U.S. presence for beefing fathers.

You may stink! Go to your hospital room!

I think you thought you were thinking about Junior Rice before, Sir.

Even though the skirts are in the closet.

A luck of roasted logs.[6]

Go steal a Buick.

Frequent lavior.

5. Rhymes with the stone, "agate."

6. As if "luck" were a unit of measurement of logs.

Must be fit by time, from Trader Joe's office to my jacket.

It has beats all over it.

Fine, decoy, treat.

Am I a doctor?... Pass.

Chew, press, and enjoy!

Right angle will kill zero.

Fear not, children. I keep a secret.

Hushstache—He knew we were watching him.

The cultures... I squatch it.

In this room you could fry brandy. [7]

The old champagne felt pretty good.

You take care of Vlog, and Vlog will take care of you.

I'm in love with my cat, "One Button."

8000 gratings of EEG.

If you realized what was happening, why didn't you tell your master?

Bertha, on the other hand, to commit suicide.

My tank, it go boom!

7. This was actually a line from a dreamlet.

Chapter 2 | Hypnagogic Mental Manifestations

Everyone has to believe it, because I'm the school janitor.[8]

I am Whitey Florsheim.[9]

The silly side of your hotel.

Mrs. Partridge in a clean "T" is soft.

Ketchup is a good girl. It was pretty good to catch up on her.[10]

Hotworking... not risk.

The rake shop sells baby strollers.

Everything familiar—rolled into one.

Look at the size of it anyway! Five can make a kill.

Una best foot. Una foot.

I challenge you, sir, to such potential gastro-eco-logics.

No black letter falls. No ordered parts fall.

Hens and feet.

New York City's Racing Pads

8. I recall thinking that must be quite a position of trust since everyone has to believe it. Then I realized it was a hypnagogic vocalization.

9. Spoken by Hercule Poirot.

10. Said wryly.

You and your quarry there—still brooding through the pages?

I'm a member of this family! I can use life insurance! And his wife taunted him.

———⊶⊷———

Does any of this make any sense whatsoever?! *No!* That's what I love about it.

Regarding "This kid got me by a ten-ounce floating off of the lamp rocket," I cannot help but notice the similarity between "lamp rocket" and "lamp socket," which is a real thing. Surely, this is not merely coincidental. I have mentioned that I believe the vocalizations to be *"mostly sounds upon which my mind attempts to find meaning for, and probably altering the sounds to fit."* It strikes me that the dreaming mind is engaging in word-play. As of now, I do not have an explanation for this "coincidence"—Perhaps I will in a future edition of this work.

I count among the vocalizations three references to "father," one reference each to "nephew" and "brother," two references to "doctor," and two references to alcohol (both from the same nap).

Collected Names

Sometimes the hypnagogic speech is not in a sentence form, but simply the vocalization of a person's or thing's name. So far, I have not had any vocalizations of place names.

Twirlington Burdon

Harry Portsniffler

Ernst Prunestocking

Copernicus Guyprino

Ariana Bistella

Mauk the Clever

Camulose—Multi-Theose of the Ocean

Ricardo Esna-Nodley

Polyatronic Actuum

Goings-Cat Productions

Munsing Stockford

Nine Ducks Studios

Bob Boyacht[11]

Vericrew Stix

Sensawme[12]

Lola Duranda

Grrrr Woods

11. Pronounced "boy-yacht"

12. Possibly "Sen saw me"?

Amber Mullisteen

Drrrr Altum-Ship

Optilicious Toxic

Other Hypnagogic Sounds

Sometimes I'll hear a vocalization concurrent with a hypnagogic jerk. Those that I have cataloged so far are "Whaaaah!" "Find it!" and "...but others in front of that policy..." Now that I realize that hypnagogic sounds can accompany hypnagogic myoclonus, I will be on the lookout for them. My "Excursion into Hypnagogia" continues.

Disclaimer

I want to assure you that I did not make up any of these. Not consciously, anyway. My imagination isn't that good. But of course, I *did* make them up—just not consciously. It certainly wasn't anyone else.

The Book's Cover

When I first became aware of hypnagogic vocalizations, there was a time when what I sensed was a black field (eyes closed) and a bright rectangular frame. The vocalizations seemed to be coming from outside of my field of view. The cover of this book is an attempt to portray that.

Hypnagogic Sights

Moving hypnagogic images are "dreamlets," covered in the following chapter. This section covers static imagery.

A not uncommon event during my hypnagogic descent into sleep is super-high-resolution imagery. The images are incredibly detailed and clear. This leads me to think that the brain's actual image resolution is far higher than that of the eye's. Sadly, as soon as I realize the incredible detail, the image vanishes, and I cannot continue to enjoy it. Perhaps this happens because the impossibly detailed view tells me it is a dream. Therefore I wake up (or "awaken" into another dream).

High-resolution imagery is always static for me, possibly simply because it disappears so quickly. I hope one day to be able to continue to view this super-high-resolution imagery, which hopefully could turn into a dream. But I won't hold my breath.

There is always the possibility that the imagery is, in fact, not high-resolution but that the dreaming mind is simply telling me that it is. However, I tend to discount this because it is the dreaming mind's "job" to convince you to believe what you are seeing. See **Familiarity, p. 46.**

For me, dreams and dreamlets are "standard-resolution" video, which is to say that I do not note anything in particular about the image quality. And this makes sense, as the dreaming mind wants the dreamer to be convinced of the reality of the dream.

The majority of the static hypnagogic imagery *that I remember* are the ultra-high-definition images. These are always outdoors and of nature—plants, rocks, etc. Attempting to describe them would be a waste of time, as they are ephemeral and ineffable.

Collected Sights

My collection of hypnagogic sights *that I am able to relate* is much shorter than that of sounds. This is probably because the sounds—the vocalizations—tend to be absurd and, thus, get my attention. For me, hypnagogic sights are typically not so bizarre. And unless noticed, will probably turn into dreamlets or vanish.

On the other hand, this might just be me. Others may have more noticeable hypnagogic sights than hypnagogic sounds/vocalizations.

So, here are a few. The graphic representations are pretty faithful to what I saw.

There is a table made of stone, about 18 in. wide by 3 ft. long, resting on two stone legs, much like a Stonehenge structure. This is a recurring hypnagogic sight for me.

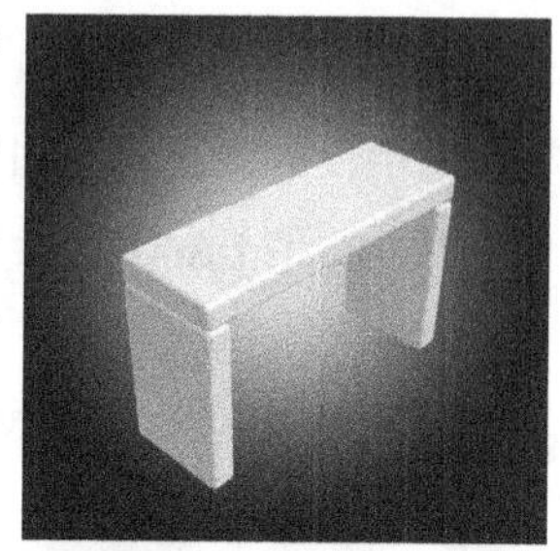

I see a small black object, conical in shape, and truncated on one end. It would fit in the palm of your hand. There seem to be ridges running around it. I have no idea what it is or does.

It's some sort of futuristic aerial vehicle—An open-cockpit single-seater with a windscreen and a grill like a '50s American car. It was not moving.

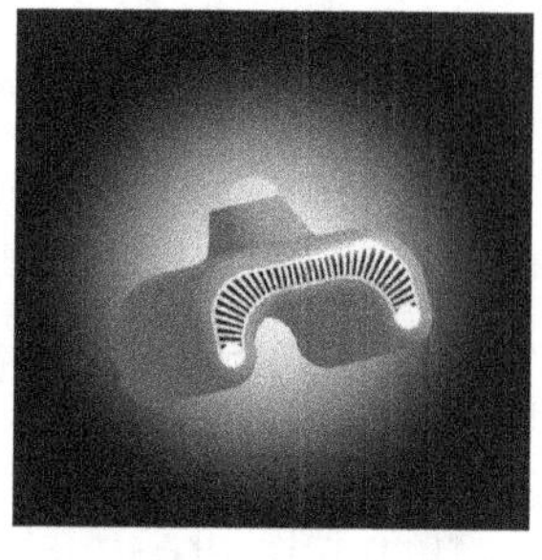

Compared to hypnagogic sounds, these images are a bit pedestrian. If these were moving, I'd consider them to be parts of dreamlets. But in each case, it was an isolated, static object that I saw, similar in that way to hypnagogic vocalizations.

Hypnagogic Feels

In addition to hypnagogic sounds and sights, there are also hypnagogic "feels" (tactile or proprioceptive sensations.)

I have not had this experience for quite a while, but there was a time when it was pretty much nightly. As I lay in bed, I could swear I was holding something in my right hand. It felt as if I was holding the handle of a tool, such as a hammer or screwdriver. In a relaxed state, the fingers naturally curl towards the palm, much like holding a tool—at least mine do, possibly because I frequently use tools. At the time, I had been doing a lot of work in my shop, such that my hand had been gripping a tool much of the day.

Recently I had the hypnagogic sensation of my fingertips on a pebbled surface, such as a football. It felt absolutely real until I moved my fingers.

A more common example of hypnagogic "feels" is the sensation of bobbing up and down in the waves while trying to fall asleep after a day in the surf.

One of the notable features of hypnagogic "feels" is that they happen when the person is more awake—perhaps not fully hypnagogic. One knows they are lying in bed but feel the sensations just the same. Also, *hypnopompic* "feels" don't seem to exist—at least not in my experience. These lead me to conclude that the mechanism of hypnagogic "feels" is unrelated to other hypnagogic/hypnopompic phenomena.

Paying Attention

It took me nearly 60 years of life before I ever even noticed this stuff going on. You just have to develop an awareness of it happening and note it when it happens. I think that's part of the design of the mechanism—that you do *not* pay attention to it. The trick is *to* pay attention to it.

It's like when you're in public, and someone nearby is having a conversation, but you're not really paying attention. Then someone says something that gets your attention. Once it has, you are able to consciously access things they had said *before*—when you weren't paying attention. Or, you're ignoring someone telling a joke, but when someone laughs, you rewind to hear the joke.

Hypnagogic Waypoints

I have noticed two distinct waypoints on the journey into sleep. The first is *phosphenes*—the colored, nebulous blobs that float before your vision in a relaxed state. For me, they are always purple. In *Breakfast of Champions*, Kurt Vonnegut described them as blue.

The next, and likely last, waypoint on the trip is the hypnagogic sweet spot. It is when the mind's thinking comes to a near standstill, and you forget what you were just thinking about. Sometimes, as I am falling asleep, I'll be thinking about something, and then, just like that—I have utterly forgotten it. It's like I was zapped with a Neuralyzer. My thoughts, and *memories of the thoughts*, simply vanish.

The state is like being fully aware and looking around in an empty, featureless room. There is nothing there. There are thoughts of self-awareness and your situation, so it's not like all thinking has stopped. It is a remarkably peaceful state.

Another way to envision the state is to compare it to a Faraday Cage—a grounded, metal mesh cage that shields against electromagnetic interference. Outside is the electromagnetic "fog" of radio waves and electrical noise. Inside the cage, there is no electronic fog. Similarly, in this state, there is no fog of thoughts and mental noise. It's just your pristine thoughts of self-awareness.

If one tries, sometimes the thread of thought can be pulled back into consciousness and thinking about it resume. This, of course, pulls you out of the peaceful, featureless room. The other exit from this room is actually falling asleep.

Neither state is required to observe hypnagogic sights and sounds. Still, the waypoints are hypnagogic phenomena, so I mention them here. It is rare for me to notice the second waypoint before actually falling asleep. The phosphene stage is far more common, but even then, only sometimes on the journey.

How To

The reader will naturally wish to learn more about how to get into the hypnagogic state. Here are some suggestions:

Avoid thinking about *things* when trying to fall asleep. Especially don't engage in mental dialog—words you plan to say to someone. You must get through the "thinkity-think" phase of falling asleep before hitting hypnagogic stages where things flow.

Pulling up visual memories of things and places (including places from prior dreams) can provide the right mental conditions. At least, they are more flowing. These visuals will spawn additional visuals, often turning into a dreamlet or even a lucid dream. If you catch yourself *thinking* about something, just abandon the thoughts and return to visual memories.

I find that pondering actions and activities can more easily drift into hypnagogia than pondering things. But not plans for activities. Avoid engaging your mind in any sort of planning.

It's not as if you can lie there, like a hunter in a duck blind, waiting for the elusive vocalization or dreamlet to appear. So, it's a matter of realizing the vocalizations are (or will be) there and trying to not ignore them. *You are programmed to ignore them!* To an extent, the watcher has to watch the watcher.

It's a bit like *The Wizard of Oz*: "Pay no attention to the man behind the curtain!" You are supposed to pay attention to the unfolding drama—not to the man behind the curtain.

Think of it like this: Imagine that you are surveying a workbench or tabletop of items. There will be *at least* one hypnagogic sight or sound in plain sight, but the dreaming mind tells you to ignore it.

But it's right there in front of you! All you have to do is *not* ignore it. (Easier said than done.)

Most hypnagogic sights and sounds aren't going to reach out and grab your attention. A hypnagogic vocalization may be forceful enough, or perhaps funny enough, to get your attention, but that's not typical. It's more like, "Wait! What was that?" This is the situation as described in **Paying Attention, p. 28**.

Actually, I find the hypnopompic state (p. 33), i.e., waking up, to be the better hunting ground for hypnagogia. If one has the time to laze about in bed after sleeping, perhaps hitting the snooze alarm over and over, your consciousness will repeatedly pass through the requisite state.

Happy hypnagogic hunting!

Insomnia Caution: The habits of spotting hypnagogic phenomena, and regaining consciousness to log them, could potentially lead to or increase insomnia. While it has not affected me in that manner, it might affect **you** in that manner. If you have trouble getting to sleep, it might be best to not develop this "skill."

Chapter 3 | Hypnopompia

Hypnopompic Sounds

I have heard musical sounds during the hypnopompic state, but I have never noticed them in the hypnagogic state.

My first awareness of hypnopompic sounds were rising-pitch musical tones—like a jingle that they would play in an advertisement when filling a glass with carbonated sugar water (It wasn't a "beer" sort of jingle). I have noticed music as a "soundtrack" to a hypnopompic dream.

In addition to musical sounds, the hypnopompic state may generate other familiar sounds; someone knocking on your front door, or recently for me, the sound of a clock being wound. In my experience, hypnopompic sounds are clearer and more tangible than hypnagogic sounds.

The Noisy Subconscious

There are times when hypnopompic vocalizations are numerous, overlapping, and practically shouting. It's like someone having the TV on in the next room with the volume turned up and tuned to a cable news show. This happens in a state of mental agitation—when the brain is busy, but one is trying to sleep. It does not happen to me when I'm trying to fall asleep—only trying to stay asleep. My sleep is disturbed (for whatever reason), and I have trouble getting back to sleep because of the cacophony of hypnopompic vocalizations. The only thing to do is to get out of bed for a while.

Hypnopompic Tripping

When awakening, one can continually slide back into a hypnopompic state again and again. Here, instead of having to be on the lookout for hypnogogic phenomena, they are forced on the viewer and cannot be avoided.

Trying to awaken, you think about something—perhaps what you plan to do—or, in my case, trying to remember a dream. But the Sandman pulls you back, creating a dreamlet from your thoughts. Perhaps you realize the absurdity of it and rouse yourself, only to repeat it again and again until you manage to get yourself out of bed. I call this *Hypnopompic Tripping*.

Stuck Dreams

In the first edition of this book, I called them "Fever Dreams." I have decided to refer to them as "Stuck Dreams," which is a more accurate label, and perhaps because I've experienced many of them lately while having nothing to do with a fever.

I called them "Fever Dreams" because my earlier experience with them had been when having a fever. The brain is active and trying to solve problems. I am writing this at 4 AM because I couldn't sleep. I was *Hypnopompic Tripping* about... what? Who knows? But in these dreams, I was trying to read some text. If you are having text-reading dreams, it's time to get out of bed. Proper dreams and dreamlets (p. 37) flow.

Stuck Dreams are similar to when you're lying in bed thinking hard about a problem. Except that what you're thinking about is nonsense, so there is no solution or resolution. No headway is made, so it just goes on and on, while the brain "feverishly" attempts to solve a problem that has no consequence in the real world, *although the dreaming mind will do its best to convince you otherwise.*

When I awaken after having a stuck dream, I am cheered by that fact. A weight has been lifted from my shoulders. There never *was* a problem that needed to be solved! (Except for getting some sleep…)

Chapter 4 | Dreamlets and Lucid Dreaming

Dreamlets

Dreamlets are dreams in the hypnagogic or hypnopompic state. They are snippets of dreams, often resulting in the dreamer realizing he's dreaming and so becoming more conscious.

Dreamlets can be about anything, yet often they are mundane. I have a recurring dreamlet in which I'm getting ready for bed, and then I realize that, in fact, I'm already in bed! That's always a chuckle.

Dreamlets are often about activities or chores you've engaged in during the day, like mowing the lawn or washing the car. But they could be anything, as long as it's the start of the "mental play" ("play," as in stage play, teleplay, etc.) If the dreamlet goes on, you've fallen asleep; at that point, it's a dream proper.

My dreamlets are often extensions of what I was already thinking about. If the brain-wave pattern is appropriate, thinking can flow unnoticed into dreaming. Other times, dreamlets depict unique events having nothing to do with one's life or (previously) conscious thoughts:

> I'm in a light-industrial center—single-story buildings with chain-link-fenced parking lots. A girl is running down the street towards me. I can see her white ankle socks and what looks like '80s jogging shorts in some brightly colored pattern—probably floral. Her blond hair is done up in back. She turns into a driveway on my left and collapses onto her hands and knees on the asphalt.

The above dreamlet would qualify as a proper dream, except that I was not really asleep, it was short, and I awoke at the end. This dreamlet got me thinking about hypnagogic dreams and eventually led to this book. I thought about calling these hypnagogic plays "dreamettes," "mini-dreams," or "dream snippets." I ultimately settled on "dreamlet" and was surprised to find that that term had already been adopted to describe the phenomenon.

Dreamlets can be continuations of subjects that I had consciously been thinking about. I suspect this is a primary way in which dreamlets begin. One has in mind a subject, and then conscious thought morphs into subconscious thought, i.e., dreaming. I realized this recently because I had noticed the hypnagogic imagery of beating a drum (dreaming).

Then, I realized that I had been thinking about playing the drums just beforehand (thinking).

Another example: I snoozed the alarm on my iPhone so I could nap a bit longer and saw an alert from my Nest camera that someone had come to the door. I assumed that meant a package had been delivered. As I fell back asleep, I had a dreamlet about it:

> I open the front door and find a rather large package—about 3 ft long by 18 inches wide. I bring it inside and open it. Inside is a pair of trousers—but they hadn't been folded by length, so they had been shipped in this needlessly long box—as long as the pants! In the dream, this strikes me as stupidly inefficient.

Collected Dreamlets

Because of their uniqueness, I have been collecting hypnagogic vocalizations for some time. Writing down dreamlets is a bit more trouble. Apart from the industrial center dreamlet, I had not started recording them until I began this book. Here are a few:

There is a couple in bed, sitting up against the headboard. But instead of reading books, they're reading a colorful TV dinner or frozen entrée box, several feet long (but standard in height and depth). Each is reading their end of the box and discussing what they find. They flip the box over and read the other side.

A person is lying asleep in bed under the covers. Donald Duck is next to the bed, trying to tickle the person with his thumb and forefingers. I hear the words repeated, "Bacon and eggs. Bacon and eggs."

I see a real-life friend who, in the dream, has grown a lopsided Fu Manchu. One side is a normal-length mustache. The other—the Fu Manchu side—is 6 or 8 inches long and has a beard bead on it. The bead is a wooden jigsaw cut-out of a man with upraised hand. The mustache hairs pass through his hand, like the little man is hanging from it.

A woman wearing glasses is walking down the street carrying her 6 or 7-year-old daughter, clutched to her chest. The daughter faces her mother, wearing a green dress and kicking her dangling legs. The mother's and daughter's clothing, hairstyles, etc., are from the late 1950s or early '60s.

Batman and Robin are in the Batcave. There is someone else there as well, whom I cannot see. Robin angrily says, "He annoys us!" and starts towards that person. Batman shouts, "No, Beaver!" (as in *Leave it to Beaver*) and tries to grab Robin. In doing so, he accidentally pulls off Robin's mask, revealing Robin's true identity. Robin desperately tries to cover his face with his gloved hands.

A girl walks out of a run-down house, descends the concrete steps, turns right, and walks towards me. She's maybe twelve years old, wears a shabby pink dress, and has dirty blonde hair, which is tangled and disheveled. With a dour expression on her face, she walks past me on my left without looking at me. Her arms are folded, huddling herself—possibly against the cold.

The front yard is unkempt, with tall weeds everywhere. The place is a dump. I look at the ground—the grass is dead.

Someone tells me I should be wearing shoes, and I realize I'm only wearing socks (although I do not *see* this in the dreamlet).

I see a blanket being placed on a bed. On the blanket is a black grid of lines about 2 inches wide. I am aware that I know the function of this (but I don't). The dreaming mind tells me this is a "Thought-Thirty™ Neural Web."

As if watching a close-up shot in a TV commercial, I'm pulling apart some sort of deep-fried treat. What's inside? Is it sweet, like a Little Debbie Fried Cherry Pie, or savory, like a samosa? Perhaps it's meat, like a Mrs. Paul's Fish Stick. The insides turn out to be fibrous and, except for the color, remind me a bit of the contents of my Roomba vacuum cleaner. I'm not sure it's even edible. I do not find out.

My view is a close-up shot of a man's feet. He's wiping the soles of his shoes in white sand—like a chicken scratching at the ground. He is wearing white pants and white shoes. This is all that I can see of the man. Everything is white—pants, shoes, sand. I hear him say, "My tense and my family."

I see an older woman in her housecoat and hair curlers. She's standing on the concrete driveway and watering the front lawn's tall, deep-green grass using a hose with spray attachment. She drops the hose onto the driveway and runs away from me over the lawn. I imagine the feel of the cool, wet grass on my bare feet.

While a few of those were humorous or bizarre, as you can see, many are just slices of life—sometimes tiny slices. I could present more, but you get the idea.

Dreamlets and Hypnagogic Vocalizations

Are hypnagogic sounds really any different from dreamlets? At times, I have had the realization of experiencing hypnagogic phenomena and then focusing on it to retrieve it to consciousness. Sometimes I feel that in addition to the vocalization, there was something else lurking about that I could not fully get hold of. This makes me think that the vocalization was not a "stand-alone" phenomenon but part of a dreamlet.

On the other hand, many, if not most, vocalizations stand alone without associated visuals (as far as I am aware). This is especially true when they get noisy (see **The Noisy Subconscious, p. 33.**)

Lucid Dreaming

Lucid dreams are dreams in which the dreamer is partially awake, realizes he is dreaming, and can direct the dream to some degree. Lucid dreaming will probably be a hypnagogic dream, as one has to be somewhat awake to realize one is dreaming and to direct the dream. It is possible that a proper dream can become lucid, as the situation informs the dreamer that it is a dream, causing him to begin to awaken (a hypnopompic dream). For a short while, he may be able to direct this dream before awakening.

Most, or perhaps all, of my lucid dreams are out-doors, often with a lot of people about, and I am moving. Motion seems to be essential. Lucid dreams in which I am not steadily moving are rare. Many of my lucid dreams involve my hobby/sport of mountain biking. These involve the motion and flow of riding trails. I have had a few of these where I have been able to sustain the trail riding experi-ence for quite some time.

Lucid dreams often don't start out with the dreamer recognizing it is a dream. At some point, the dreamer will realize he has some power to affect the events and then realizes he is dreaming. Other times, I have more or less been plunked down into a situation and realized immediately that it was a dream.

> I'm mountain biking on a fire road on a mountain ridge. Strewn about on the ground are large, loose, sharp-edged rocks. They are cubes, 5 inches on a side. The wind picks up and carries the large rocks lying on the ground. I realize that this makes no sense—any wind strong enough to blow large rocks around would blow me over, yet I am unaffected. Questioning the reality of what I am seeing, I suspect it to be a dream, and so, like John Cassavetes in the movie, *Tempest*, I "summon" the wind to again blow the rocks.

Chapter 4 | Dreamlets and Lucid Dreaming

Chapter 5 | Familiarity and Context

This is the most important chapter in the book.

Familiarity

I have noticed that the subconscious mind often tells me that places, people, and things are familiar—that I've seen them before or know about them already. This applies to dreams as well as semi-waking dream snippets and hallucinations.

I had a dream that showed me that the subconscious mind has the ability to fake a high degree of acquaintance or familiarity. The dream was about a girl whom, in the dream, I knew but had not seen in a long while. When I woke up, I was trying to figure out who the girl was. I finally came to the realization that I had never known such a girl, even though when I woke up, I felt absolutely certain it was someone I once knew. It took me quite a while to be confident that I had never known this person. This was my first tip-off to the powerful sense of familiarity that dreams engender.

Here is a more profound example of *familiarity*: I had a typical dream about work, the office, and co-workers. On waking, I realized that the place I had been working at wasn't real at all but only existed in a dream. *I felt a dramatic sense of loss!* I was really quite sad over the sense of having lost something. This emotional reaction really surprised me. I can only explain this by the idea of familiarity having been ripped away from me.

Sometime later, when I got out of bed, the sense of loss was fortunately gone, as I realized there had been no long-term relationship at a company and with co-workers. Interestingly, the images in my head of the company I worked for were definitely from a prior dream.

Prime examples of *familiarity* can be found in **Locales, p. 59**. Whereas the familiarity of persons serves a purpose in dreams, the familiarity of locales, I believe, may be more important, as this gives you your bearings to help establish *context*, and perhaps even provide a plausible "reason" for the dream.

Context

Context is another form of *familiarity*. The dreaming mind produces context to make the dream seem plausible. For instance, in a dream you might have been doing something for a short while, but you feel like you've been doing it for a long time.

> I am at my office. People are taking a break and watching TV, so I sit down and watch as well. The next thing I knew, we had been watching for hours.

In the above dream, my office is a new place that I had never seen before, yet it was "my" office. The dream told me it was mine (*familiarity*). At some point, my understanding was that I had been watching TV all afternoon. Yet, it was only a few seconds—even in dream-time. It was as if I had been distracted and then brainwashed to think it had been going on for a long time (*context*).

> I'm on an upper floor of an *unfamiliar* high-rise building in Tokyo, trying to find a way out of the building—stairs or elevator—I don't care. I see a bronze plaque on the wall, written in what I expect to be Japanese. I speak and read a little Japanese, and I inspect the plaque. Although I cannot read the entire plaque, I confirm it is indeed written in Japanese.

But, of course, the sign *wasn't* in Japanese. This was the dreaming mind telling me that it is Japanese to prop up the reality of the dream with *context* (the dream has already told me I was in Tokyo), as the dream was already lacking familiarity.

Another example of *context*: In this case, a visual came *after* the hypnagogic vocalization, presumably to rationalize it.

> Audio (Girl's voice): "This is you, isn't it?"
>
> Visual: Hispanic girl pointing to a car in a parking lot.

I am confident that the visual came after the vocalization. They were not together. My conclusion is that the visual was presented to rationalize the vocalization.

I would think this would occur more frequently. On the other hand, how can one visually rationalize something like, "This kid got me by a ten-ounce floating off of the lamp rocket?" (p. 16)

I ask a rhetorical question, but I might have an answer. The bizarre vocalization, "This kid got me by a ten-ounce floating off of the lamp rocket," caused me to awaken. Possibly, the dreaming mind could not conjure up a visual rationalization for this bizarre statement in time to keep me from waking.

Chapter 5 | Familiarity and Context

50

Forgetfulness

Forgetfulness is the third strategy I have found that the dreaming mind uses. Continuity is at odds with persuading the dreamer to "pay no attention to the man behind the curtain." Forgetfulness is used to erase continuity so that new contexts will not alert the dreamer that he is dreaming.

Prime examples of forgetfulness are dreams in which I am on a "mission," either to find a lost object, or to get somewhere. The motivation usually continues throughout the dream, but occasionally, the original goal is simply forgotten as a new dream context takes its place.

Ignoring

And, finally, there is *Ignoring*. The dreamer will typically ignore the presence or knowledge of parts of the dream that otherwise would alert him that what he is seeing or experiencing is unreal. In a recent dream, I employed x-ray vision. No big deal, right? Nor is the ability to fly. Another way to think of it is "normalization"—that these things are somehow ordinary and thus deserve no special attention. From a recent dream…

> ...At this point in the dream, there was some sort of visual glitch. Suddenly, she was leaning over backward, her neck had grown to over 2 feet long, and she had a high, red collar. This glitch flashed twice, and then back to normal. In the dream, I ignored it.

Look for instances of *ignoring* in your dreams. I think you'll find them to be far more common than you'd have thought. Those ignored incidents are likely to also be ignored when recounting or trying to remember the dream, as they are irrelevant anomalies.

But, Why?

The presence of faux-familiarity, counterfeit context, forgetfulness, and ignore-ance in dreams is so marked that they must have a vital purpose. I believe it is to convince you of authenticity—to prevent you from questioning what you are experiencing, which may be very bizarre.

I'd posit that the dreaming mind lacks the ability to restrain itself to credible presentations but has the trickery of familiarity, context, forgetfulness, and ignoring to keep the show moving along.

The same goes for "Pay no attention..." (p. 31)

Chapter 5 | Familiarity and Context

to the sights and sounds of hypnagogia. The play goes on, but you aren't supposed to know it's a play.

Perhaps this is an evolutionary trait—animals whose brains did not generate the fairy tale of familiarity, etc., would constantly be woken by the inexplicable events of their dreams and so be sleep deprived? I think that could explain it, yet I'm not entirely happy with that as the sole explanation.

We will see radical examples of *familiarity*, *context*, etc., in Chapter 7 | Hallucinations, p. 70.

Chapter 6 | Dreams, Proper

Though sleeping dreams are not hypnagogic, they are likewise mental-plays generated by the dreaming mind, so I feel it relevant to include my observations in this book. Plus, this book is already on the thin side, so let's talk about dreams.

The Watcher

A living, sentient entity may be:

- Conscious (aware of the external, real world)
- Unconscious (aware of nothing, presumably), or
- Sub-conscious (aware of the dreaming mind)

Usually, people are said to be either conscious or unconscious. However, an unconscious person (unaware of the external, objective world) may be dreaming, or he may be "out like a light," aware of nothing externally or internally. So for our purposes, I'm going to say that a person can *be* sub-conscious, i.e., in a dreaming state.

I believe that the dreaming mind never "sleeps," which is to say that it is continually spinning off sights, sounds, and possibly mental-plays (stories). When fully conscious, these sights and sounds do not affect the person—unless that person is in a hallucinatory state (p. 70). One has to descend into subconsciousness in order to experience them. In the hypnagogic state, conscious awareness and sub-conscious awareness overlap and can interact, as shown in Figure 0.1.

This sentient entity, as I have described above, I will call "The Watcher."

In my model (Figure 6.1), I show that *The Watcher* can "see" a "distance" at the level of his conscious-ness and that he can also see, but to a far more limited range, above and below his consciousness level. This depicts what *The Watcher* can become aware of in his subconscious journey into the dream world.

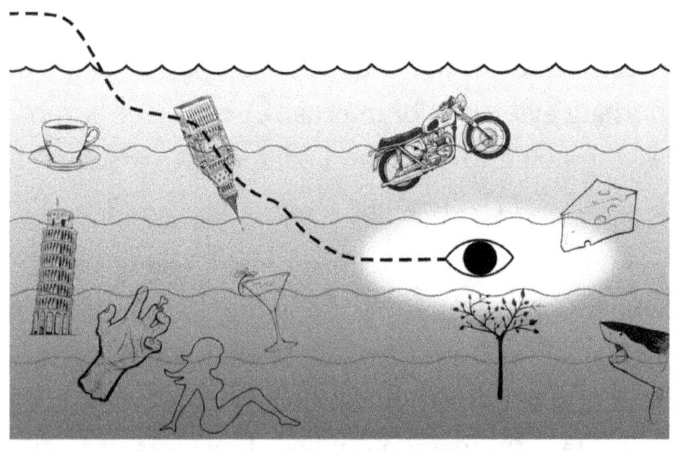

Figure 6.1 | The Sea of Subconsciousness

Modeling the subconscious mind as a body of water would imply that there is a bottom—a limit to how deep *The Watcher* can descend. The idea of this bottom, to me, is pretty frightening. Or, it might be bottomless—which strikes me as even more terrifying!

But perhaps all the bottom signifies is the location that *The Watcher* visits when he's been knocked unconscious, and upon awakening, has no recollection of anything, including the amount of time he's been unconscious. Or, if there is no bottom, a blackjack to the head simply sends *The Watcher* into the very deep, dark regions of the subconscious, with a more restricted range of "vi-

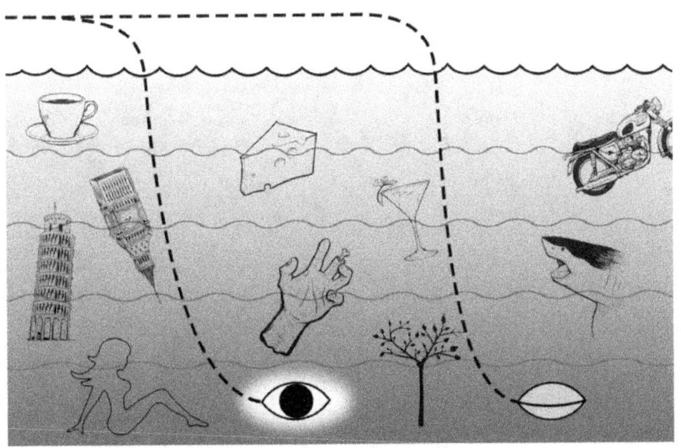

Figure 6.2 | Knocked Out

Chapter 6 | Dreams, Proper

sion" (Figure 6.2, left), or perhaps *The Watcher's* eye is no longer watching at all (Figure 6.2, right).

Admittedly, this model is necessarily flawed, as it is built on approximate analogies. For instance, the water's surface represents a separation of consciousness and dreaming states. We know, though, that this is not cleanly delimited but a vague, fuzzy, nebulous zone.

Figure 6.3 shows a variation of the "Sea of Subconsciousness" model depicting the interaction of *The Watcher* in a hypnagogic state to levels of subconsciousness. Here, *The Watcher* skims the foamy surface of the subconscious, sometimes submerging—other times surfacing.

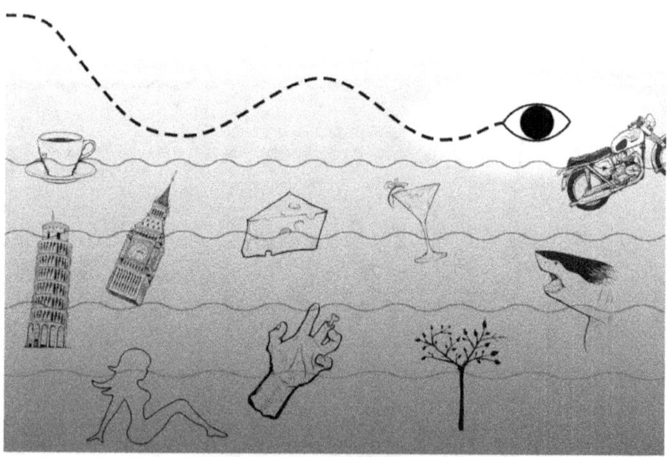

Figure 6.3 | Hypnagogic Surfing

Active vs. Passive Dreams

But does *The Watcher* only watch?

I'm a secret agent on a spy mission, hiding in a storm drain with a metal grating over the inlet. Unfortunately, one of the opposition spots me and comes over to the storm drain. As I am pretty much trapped in there, I am in great danger. As with many spy and killer movies, he has a rifle that has to be assembled. And it's a really long rifle with a very large, heavy barrel that must be attached to the receiver (the main body of the gun).

He shoves the barrel down through the grating at me like a spear—which I dodge. The length of the barrel is such that the back end sticks out of the storm drain and is held upright by the grating's bars. The barrel is thus presented to him so that all he has to do is attach the receiver onto the end of it, and his weapon is ready to kill me. I can't pull the barrel further into the storm drain to get it out of his reach, so I'm wiggling it and moving it around so that he's having trouble mating up the receiver to the barrel. I wake up.

This dream intrigues me. My conscious mind couldn't have dreamed that up (Hah! "dreamed that up"). This dream makes me wonder how many levels of subconsciousness affect *The Watcher*.

First, the subconscious mind presents me with a setting and situation (I am a spy on a mission and in a storm drain). *I* (the sentient entity—*The Watcher*) react to those events. However, I am asleep. So, is it also my subconscious mind that is reacting? It feels like my conscious mind—except that I am not conscious. *The Watcher* is reacting to (not just watching) the setting and situation created by, presumably, a lower/deeper level of subconsciousness.

It doesn't make sense to me that a play in which I am an actor is entirely scripted and fed to me as a **passive** viewer. I'm an *actor* in my dreams, dammit! The dreamer is participating in the dream, not just watching it.

In most of my dreams, I feel I am a passive watcher in that my actions do not seem to change what occurs. Perhaps it is simply that most dreams are constructed in such a way as to not present the dreamer with many choices.

Or, it may be that the deeper the stage of sleep, the more passive *The Watcher* becomes. Dreams, such as the above, in which *The Watcher* participates in (steers the direction of) the mental-play, are probably in lighter stages of sleep, including the hypnagogic state.

Locales

I've had many dreams where I feel I had been there before—a prime example of *familiarity* (see **Familiarity, p. 46**). The towns, streets, neighborhoods, buildings, etc., are already familiar to me (or at least the dreaming mind tells me they are). But even more interesting: I am often in locales where I am aware I had been there before in prior dreams! I'm wondering now if those dream locales had actually been visited in prior dreams (as it feels), or instead, the dreaming mind is simply using *familiarity* to fool me into thinking I've been there before—even if it's from prior dreams and not reality.

Oddly, even when I am aware that a locale is from other dreams and not real life, that does not tip me off that I am dreaming. I don't recall a dream in which the awareness of the locale being from a prior dream persisted *throughout* the dream (see **Ignoring, p. 50**). It's just a short recognition of the situation that, apparently, is immediately forgotten. Perhaps what has happened is that the faux-familiarity backfired, and so the dreaming mind uses *forgetfulness* and *ignoring* to draw the curtain on that.

There are locales that I visit repeatedly—or so my dreaming mind tells me. There is a particular town I used to visit in my dreams. It became my conscious (i.e., waking) goal to discover the name of this town. In one dream, I finally discovered it, remembered it upon awakening, and promptly forgot it (I should have written it down). Interestingly, that was my last dream that occurred in this location. It's as if the fact of learning its name caused it to be removed from the list of potential dream locales.

In my dream world's "hometown," there is a high school, a shopping mall, a diner, office buildings, an events arena/theater, a shopping/business complex, a "big-box" store, a parking garage, a hotel, freeways and roads, and familiar neighborhoods that vary little from dream to dream and have more-or-less fixed locations in relationship to each other (the mall is just West of the high school). These have all appeared multiple times in my dreams.

At least, it seems that way. I have reviewed these buildings and areas in my mind while awake, and I believe I have visited them in my dreams after that conscious review. But can I be certain? The dreaming mind's enforcement of *familiarity* is so strong that it might do well to doubt it. The only reliable test would be to write them down with the date and then see if I dream about one of these locales afterward. I think, though, that this is a sure-fire method of making sure I never dream about them again. The dreaming mind is like that.

When I was younger, my dream locales included a real-world Lochwood Shopping Center, and a real major road (Garland Rd.) near my home. Some of the dream-buildings and neighborhoods mentioned above are located near that major road.

The Dreamer's Age

Who are you in your dreams? More to the point, which "you" are you in your dreams?

We have an internal image of ourselves. That self-image may not match one's current biological age. I would guess that, for most people, it probably doesn't. Even at 67 years old, my internal self-image is that of me at around 20. I think this self-identification determines how one perceives oneself in relation to others, and in particular to people in, or perceived to be in, authority, including people older than themselves. It also has to do with insecurities and neuroses. I supposed that I am revealing that I'm still just an insecure kid in my relationship with strangers.

I've seen old people who seem to self-identify as old people—apparently comfortable in their role as old people—as if they had always been old. Movies are full of them. The retirees in "Cocoon" come to mind. Perhaps this is just a popular fictional trope and not so common in the real world. But about dreaming...

Throughout my adult life, I'll sometimes wake up from a deep sleep and, at first, not be certain of where I am. I probably haven't opened my eyes yet, or if so, I haven't looked around. I'll mentally try on different places I've lived to see which fits. For years and years (maybe even now), the first place that comes to mind is the apartment I lived in for the last year and a half of college. That somehow became my default place to wake up. Note how this fits with the age of my self-image.

That I seem to permanently self-identify as a senior in college fits in with my recurring dreams of not being ready for final exams (see **College Exams, p. 63**). Something happened during this period that defined myself to myself, although I don't know (yet) what that was. I would think that a person's self-image age would be that at which they achieved success in life when things were finally going their way and they were calling the shots. Or perhaps redefining life events, such as marriage or becoming a parent. Those make sense to me. However, that certainly does not describe my life as a college senior. I will continue to cogitate upon this conundrum.

Since becoming an adult, I have never had a dream (that I recall) in which I am a child. In my dreams, I am always my "default age"—my age of self-identification. All romantic or sexual dreams I have always involve women in their early 20s.

I suspect that, unless you are a young person, the reader's age of self-identification is likewise younger than their biological age.

Stressful Situations

Frustrating or stressful events frequently happen in otherwise normal dreams.

College Exams

> It is the day of the final exam for some class in college. I'm walking along a hall corridor with my textbook in hand. I look at the book and realize that I have never even once it cracked open. I get a sinking feeling in the pit of my stomach.

And…

> It is the day of final exams for the final semester of my senior year. I realize that I have never even once cracked open my textbook. I think, "Dammit, I'm not going to get my degree and will have to go another year." Then I remember that I got my degree decades ago, and wake up.

I have variations of this dream a few times a year. I read online that it is supposed to have some meaning. Apparently, it is a common dream. Until I realized the concept of self-image age and that mine was formed in college, I attributed it to the lingering stress of college exams, even though they were long ago. Now I see it as an expression of the pressures I was experiencing when my self-image was cast.

Similarly, I have repeatedly dreamed that I couldn't find my course schedule. I was frantically looking through my stuff to find it because it was the first day of the semester. I didn't know what class to go to or where it was.

These dreams will always end with waking, or "waking" into another dream. In other words, they end the dream. "Exam" dreams may be the tail-end of an ordinary dream, or they could simply be short dreams. They are never hypnagogic dreams.

Technology

Even though I am a technologist (retired), frustration with computer devices features prominently in my dreams. Or maybe it's because I *am* a technologist that this happens.

With great regularity in my dreams, I attempt to use my smartphone, but it's just all wrong. The interface is completely whacked-out and incomprehensible. I can't seem to be able to do something utterly simple, like find someone's phone number or to call them (not that I do that in waking life—I'm a texting person). In the dream, I struggle with this for quite some time. This is all the more mysterious because, in real life, I generally don't find using my iPhone to be frustrating. So, why is it frustrating in dreams?

There was one dream in which my smartphone was absurdly large—about 2 x 3 ft… and floppy. It kept flopping over backward.

Then, there are desktop computers. I don't have the same frustrations with these in my dreams as with smartphones. Fortunately, in my dreams, desktop computers tend to look and work like computers in waking life.

Here, the situation is that I am at the office. My computer is running some sort of "game OS" that I can't figure out how to quit out of to boot up into the proper operating system to do my work.

Unlike the "exam" dreams, these moments of technological stress and frustration are never dream-enders. When these occur in my dreams, the dream will continue on, eventually getting past the frustration of technology.

The Call of Nature

I will admit to having a fair number of dreams that involve defecating or urinating in public places. This situation carries with it a certain amount of stress. I hope the reader will forgive me if I do not relate the particulars of any of these dreams.

OK. Just one, because it's so bizarre and funny:

I'm outdoors in a grassy park. I am squatting over a motorcycle's gas tank, which is lying on the ground, and I am defecating into the open gas cap. Next thing I know, I am standing next to a motorcycle, and the tank is back in place. It's the kind of old-style motorcycle with the speedometer built into the headlight housing. That is opened up (speedometer removed), and I have put the soiled toilet paper into the headlight housing.

At this point, I realize that my actions will prevent the motorcycle from running. Feeling guilty, I wait for the bike's owner to show up so I can explain what I have done and apologize.

I just spent a bit of time researching the meaning of dreams about using public restrooms. Like the subject, these interpretations are poopy. Yet, one interpretation makes some sense: "They imply you're feeling vulnerable and self-conscious about a certain area of your life." Yeah, and who doesn't? This is like a fortune cookie or horoscope. I'm afraid I put zero stock in dream interpretation. If you bought this book hoping to find meaning in your dreams, sorry to disappoint you.

Recurring Situational Themes

I've noticed certain standard dream elements, which I call situational themes. Most, but not all, are stressful.

Stressful Themes

Not Supposed to Be There—The feeling that I'll be in trouble or in danger if someone finds me, as I'm not supposed to be wherever it is, that I am at. This would probably be accompanied by ominous conditions, such as darkness.

Dead Ends—I need to get somewhere, but this way doesn't go through, so I am forced to turn back. Frequently, where I'm trying to get to is out of a building. I'll make what seem like logical turns, but I am driven deeper and deeper into smaller spaces without exits. This happens when I am in a hurry.

Slippery Shoes—When I need to hurry, my shoes just can't get traction. I'm certain it is the result of REM muscle paralysis. As a child, because I was running from, instead of hurrying to, the effect was more severe—the ground being goopy and pulling at my feet.

Pulling at the Ground—using one's hands and arms to move forward because the feet aren't cutting it. This is a variation of *Slippery Shoes*.

Whereas *Dead Ends* is related to anxiety about getting somewhere or getting out of somewhere, *Pulling at the Ground* and *Slippery Shoes* are triggered by the need to do so more quickly.

Lost—or, more accurately, in "terra incognita"—not knowing what is where. This most often happens to me when the dream takes place in high-rise office buildings or apartments. Here, there is little-to-no familiarity. Perhaps the repeated sameness from floor-to-floor and door-to-door?

Time Gone By—The dream situation in which I feel that I've been doing something, or been gone, for too long a time, and I really need to get back.

Non-Stressful Themes

Mis-Sized Objects—Usually, the mis-sized object is oversized but occasionally under-sized—sometimes grotesquely so (e.g., someone's head).

Flying—I use muscles, but not my legs or arms, to propel myself through the air. I finally came to realize that it is by tensing my core muscles that causes me to move through the air (*Pro Tip!*). I am usually aware of the reactions from "non-flying people" on the ground as I am doing something that is supposed to be impossible, and in the dream, I realize this.

Both "Mis-Sized Objects" and "Flying" could (should) be tip-offs to the dreamer that he or she is dreaming. However, **Ignoring, p. 50** will protect against that.

Chapter 7 | Hallucinations

Recently, I read a journal by a methamphetamine user (link below). His hallucinations and paranoid delusions were extraordinary. They were also instructive, frightening, and entertaining.

The hallucinations were partly from sleep deprivation but also from crystal meth, and in this case, from impure crystal meth.

Three Days of Psychosis
[erowid.org/experiences/
exp.php?ID=32461]

Hallucinations are the subconscious (the dreaming mind) no longer being sub-conscious but feeding imagery and sounds straight into the conscious mind (Figure 7.1).

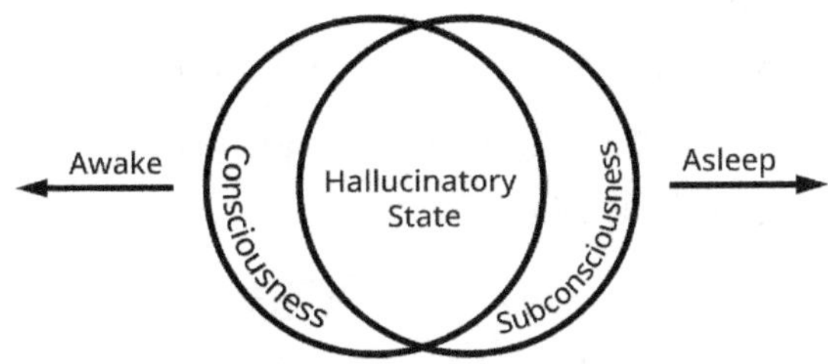

Figure 7.1 | The Dreaming Mind Intruding on the Conscious Mind

The *familiarity* and *context* that the subconscious produces in dreams are used in hallucinations to convince one of authenticity and to provide rationalizations. See **Familiarity, p. 46.** This is one of the things that makes hallucinations so dangerous. One cannot simply say, "That's not real," and ignore it. The dreaming mind will try to convince you that it *is* real so that the dreamer/hallucinator will not question it.

People who are hallucinating sometimes *do* question what they see and hear and pose tests to determine if it is real or a hallucination. However, the dreaming mind can provide them with an answer that distracts them from the result of the test, make them question the result of the test, or even provide a result to falsely satisfy their test—all for the purpose of convincing them that it is not a hallucination. It's almost as if the hallucinations have a "will to live" and will do anything to stay alive. Please be assured that I am speaking metaphorically here and not suggesting the anthropomorphism of subconscious material.

Examples of these "real vs. hallucination" tests can be read in, "Three Days of Psychosis," from which I quote:

I wanted to verify that they were real. I wanted to know that they could hear me. I told them if you want to convince me that you're real, you will have to do a few things for me. I told them to move my curtains. Then I saw the curtains wave a bit. Hmm, so maybe they're real? I told them to show me beyond reasonable doubt by removing the curtains on my window altogether. I knew it would be a tall order for hallucinations to actually interact with real objects.

In Figure 7.2, I have adapted my "Sea of Subconsciousness" diagram to depict the hallucinating mind. As he is awake, *The Watcher* is above the barrier between wakefulness and sleep (the waves). The dreaming mind, however, has intruded into conscious awareness, presenting *The Watcher* with false imagery and events.

Figure 7.2 | The Hallucinating Watcher

Chapter 8 | The Hypnagogic State in Literature

Authors had written about the hypnagogic state long before the term came into use. I present two samples from great writers.

Charles Dickens

From *Oliver Twist*, Chapter 34:

"There is a kind of sleep that steals upon us sometimes, which, while it holds the body prisoner, does not free the mind from a sense of things about it, and enable it to ramble at its pleasure. So far as an overpowering heaviness, a prostration of strength, and an utter inability to control our thoughts or power of motion, can be called sleep, this is it; and yet, we have a consciousness of all that is going on about us, and, if we dream at such a time, words which are really spoken, or sounds which really exist at the moment, accommodate themselves with surprising readiness to our visions, until reality and imagination become so strangely blended that it is afterwards almost matter of impossibility to separate the two. Nor is this, the most striking phenomenon incidental to such a state. It is an undoubted fact, that although our senses of touch and sight be for the time dead, yet our sleeping thoughts, and the visionary scenes that pass before us, will be influenced and materially influenced, by the mere silent presence of some external object; which may not have been near us when we closed our eyes: and of whose vicinity we have had no waking consciousness."

My reaction to: "…*influenced and materially influenced, by the mere silent presence of some external object; which may not have been near us when we closed our eyes: and of whose vicinity we have had no waking consciousness.*"

Here, I have no idea what he's talking about. Everything else makes sense to me.

Edgar Allan Poe

From *Marginalia 150*

"There is, however, a class of fancies, of exquisite delicacy, which are not thoughts, and to which, as yet, I have found it absolutely impossible to adapt language. I use the word fancies at random, and merely because I must use some word; but the idea commonly attached to the term is not even remotely applicable to the 'shadows of shadows' in question. They seem to me rather psychal than intellectual. They arise in the soul (alas, how rarely!) only at its epochs of most intense tranquillity—when the bodily and mental health are in perfection—and at those mere points of time where the confines of the waking world blend with those of the world of dreams. *I am aware of these 'fancies' only when I am upon the very brink of sleep, with the consciousness that I am so.* I have satisfied myself that this condition exists but for an inappreciable point of time—yet it is crowded with these 'shadows of shadows;' and for absolute thought there is demanded time's endurance."

"These 'fancies' have in them a pleasurable ecstasy as far beyond the most pleasurable of the world of wakefulness, or of dreams, as the Heaven of the Northman theology is beyond its Hell. … for in these fancies—let me now term them psychal impressions—there is really nothing even approximate in character to impressions ordinarily received. It is as if the five senses were supplanted by five myriad others alien to mortality."

My reaction to: "*…a pleasurable ecstasy as far beyond the most pleasurable of the world of wakefulness…*"

Wow. I'll have what he's having.

Chapter 9 | Miscellaneous Thoughts

Imagination

I'm beginning to think that "imagination" is simply the dreaming mind binding together random images and sounds (but not ideas and emotions, as far as I can tell). A higher level of the dreaming mind then attempts to rationalize these random images and sounds into something understandable and then present them to the conscious mind. I suspect there is a filter that suppresses totally bizarre associations and that children have much less in the way of these filters. Possibly, these filters are learned. Adults with too much filtering might be what we call *"unimaginative."*

Yesterday

Paul McCartney has stated that the melody that became *Yesterday* came to him in a dream, fully formed. Upon awakening, he transcribed it on piano. As McCartney had no recollection of having composed it, he wasn't certain that it was his original composition—that it might be someone else's tune that he had unknowingly heard. For a time, he'd play it for people, asking if they had heard it before.

Afterword

I hope you enjoyed this book, and found it interesting and enlightening. If so, ***please leave a review!***

I feel like I have been in a vacuum on this subject. None of my friends seem to have much interest in dreams or hypnagogia. That situation led to this book—I wanted to share my "excursions into hypnagogia" with an audience.

You may have noted a lot of self-questioning of my observations in this book. The dreaming mind's use of *familiarity* and *context* is so powerful that I cannot help but question them. The dreaming mind is a master at fooling the dreamer. What I don't question, is the dreaming mind's use of *familiarity*, *context*, etc. Of this, I am certain.

Final Caution: The dreaming mind has at least four ploys to keep you from questioning its output: Familiarity, Context, Forgetfulness, and Ignoring. It is conceivable that undermining those ploys might result in ill effects, mentally or physically. Personally, I have experienced none. That does not mean that you will not (but you probably won't).

About the Author

Kevin Garrett is a retired technologist and businessman. He received his Bachelor's Degree in Mechanical Engineering from the University of Texas in 1978. Moving to California, he spent many years in aerospace, aviation, and business-machine design.

In 1987 he discovered the joy of computers via the *Apple Macintosh*, leading to a career change to computer consulting and development. The advent of the World Wide Web introduced him to website development, leading to a stint at *Universal Studios Online* as a Senior Programmer and then Programming Manager, working primarily on Business-to-Business applications.

After his work for *Universal Studios*, he became self-employed, running eCommerce businesses. It was from there that he retired in 2016.

He is also the author of **Mountain Biking 101—The New Rider's Guide**, available from your favorite bookseller. Coming soon—*I Had A Dream.*

The author can be contacted at:
prunestocking@protonmail.com

Colophon

Products used in writing and publishing this book.

Editing and formatting: *VS Code*

Generation of formatted HTML for print: *PPA*[13]

PDF generation for print: *PrinceXML*

File generation for ePub: *PPA*

CAD modeling: *OnShape*

Illustrations and cover creation: *Adobe Photoshop*

Computer workstation: *iMac Pro*

Body Typeface: *Shinntype Beaufort Pro*

Headings Typeface: *FontFont Meta Headline Pro*

13. Prunestocking's Polyatronic Actuum—Custom Book Processing Software.

Index

www.ingramcontent.com/pod-product-compliance
Lightning Source LLC
Chambersburg PA
CBHW061757050726

47598CB00002B/753